The Best of 606 AGGIE JOKES

A collection of the best of the Six Volumes of **101 Aggie Jokes** and its descendents.

Published by THE GIGEM PRESS

First Printing, October, 1976
Second Printing, June, 1978
Third Printing, October, 1980

The Best of 606 Aggie Jokes, Copyright © 1980 by the Gigem Press. Published by
Gigem Press, P.O. Box 64445, Dallas Texas 75206.
Printed in U.S.A.

FOREWORD

Thanks to our readers, eight "generations" of **101 Aggie Joke Books** have been published since the first in the series came off the presses in November, 1965. The birth of succeeding volumes, from **Son of 101 Aggie Jokes** to **Great-Great-Great Grandson of 101 Aggie Jokes,** took place at two-year intervals.

As the title indicates, **The Best of 606 Aggie Jokes** contains what we think are the funniest of the jokes published in the first six books. Actually, however, they are the best of many, many more than 606 Aggie jokes. For every joke selected for publication in our books, dozens were discarded because they did not come up to our standards of humor or guidelines of good taste.

Of course, humor is a very personal thing, and it is possible that your favorite jokes do not appear here. If so, send them to us, and if we agree that they are as funny or funnier than those published in our previous books, we will send you a copy of the next volume of Aggie jokes when it is published.

The Best of 606 Aggie Jokes is gratefully dedicated to all of you who requested that we assemble our funniest into one convenient book. We hope you enjoy it and make it possible for us to publish **The Best of 1,212 Aggie Jokes** after another decade.

THE GIGEM PRESS

QUESTION: Why do haircuts cost four dollars at Aggie-land?
ANSWER: The charge is one dollar per corner.

An Aggie was sitting at a bar and happened to overhear a conversation next to him.

Eager to be friendly, he leaned over interrupting the group and said, "You fellas are from Harvard aren't you?"

"Yes we are," answered one annoyed young man, "how did you know?"

"Oh, I could tell by the suit you wear and the nasal way you talk," said the Aggie brightly.

"You're from Texas A&M," retorted the man.

"By golly, you're right," said the astonished Aggie, "How could you tell?"

"I saw your class ring while you were picking your nose."

QUESTION: Do you know the difference between a blue-eyed Aggie and a brown-eyed Aggie?
ANSWER: The blue-eyed Aggie is one quart low.

HOUSE DETECTIVE: Are you entertaining a woman in your room?
AGGIE: Just a minute. I'll ask her.

It looked like the car was stranded on a lonely road, so the farmer pulled up alongside and asked, "What's the matter? Out of gas?"

"No," came the answer from the Aggie inside.

"Engine trouble?"

"No."

"Tire down?"

"No, didn't have to."

When the marriage ceremony was over, the Aggie and his lovely bride went to a resort hotel to spend their honeymoon. Bedtime came and the bride retired, but the groom stood by the window gazing at the moon and stars.

"Dear," the bride called, "why don't you come to bed?"

Answered the Aggie, "Mother told me that tonight would be the most wonderful night of my life, and I'm not going to miss a minute of it."

_____

TESSIE: Would you like to see where I was operated on for appendicitis?

AGGIE: No. I hate hospitals.

_____

Then there was the Aggie who thought his sister was a very good girl when she came home from a week-end trip with a Gideon Bible in her handbag.

How does an Aggie tie his shoe?

A cannibal went to a new jungle restaurant for dinner and asked to see the menu. After studying it, he called the head waiter over.

"I don't understand these prices," the cannibal explained. "I see here that you're charging $2.00 for fried queen, $3.50 for roast king and $7.50 for baked Aggie. Why is baked Aggie the highest priced entree on the menu? Aggies aren't scarce."

"But sir," asked the head waiter, "did you ever try to clean one?"

1st Aggie: Did you hear the latest? The administration is trying to stop necking.
2nd Aggie: Gee, I hope they don't expect the students to stop, too!

Did you hear about the Aggie who called his girl friend to see if she was doing anything that night. She said she wasn't, so he took her out. Sure enough, she wasn't.

An Aggie went to heaven, but was stopped by St. Peter when he started to enter the section occupied by University of Texas exes.

St. Peter cautioned, "You must not go in there, son. It might cause trouble. You see, that section of heaven is reserved for former University of Texas students."

"Gosh, I'm surprised you practice segregation up here," the Aggie replied, "I thought college feuding ended a long time ago and everybody gets along with each other now. Why, I visited the University of Texas campus myself and lit the pre-Thanksgiving Day bonfire."

"Really? When was that?" St. Peter asked.

"About ten minutes ago."

After finishing his Army training, the Aggie was shipped out and wrote home, "Dear Folks, I'm not allowed to tell you where I am, but yesterday I shot a polar bear."

A few months later he wrote, "Dear Folks, our outfit was transferred and I still can't tell you where I am, but last night I danced with a hula girl."

A couple of weeks later he wrote again, "Dear Folks, I still can't tell you where I am, but today the doctor told me I should have danced with the polar bear and shot the hula girl."

The Texas Aggie was taking a lot of kidding from the citizens in the Golden Nugget Saloon in Nome, Alaska.

"We may not be the biggest state in the Union anymore but we're still the toughest," declared the Aggie.

"You must be kidding," whooped the Alaskans. "We Alaskans can't be beat when it comes to toughness. Every man here can drink a fifth of whiskey in one gulp, wrestle a grizzly bear barehanded and make love to an Eskimo woman all in one night.

"Shucks, any Texan can do that, especially an Aggie," was the retort. "I'll show you."

Whereupon he ordered a fifth of whiskey, downed it forthwith, then announced he was going out to find a bear.

A couple of hours later the Aggie staggered through the door his clothes in tatters and his body covered with cuts and bruises.

"Okay, men," bellowed the Aggie, "now where's that woman you want me to wrestle?"

Three men were registering for rooms at a hotel.
The first man signed his name on the register with an LL.B. behind it.

The desk clerk asked, "What does the L.L.B. stand for?"

"I'm a graduate of Harvard Law School, and the initials indicate that I have earned my degree as a Bachelor of Law," he explained.

The second man signed the register, and added the initials B.J. The clerk asked him what they meant and he answered that he was a graduate of the University of Missouri where he received a Bachelor of Science in Journalism degree.

The third man signed his name with an S.I.

"What on earth does S.I. mean?" the desk clerk asked.

"Why son, I'm a graduate of Texas A&M," the Ex-aggie replied, "And I got my degree in civil engineering."

After six losing seasons, the Aggie football coach was at the end of his rope. If he didn't redeem himself this season, it would be curtains for him. Desperately he sought ways to inspire his players and decided to give prayer a chance.

Accordingly, before the kick-off of the first game of the season, the Aggie team assembled on the field, knelt, and the coach led them in prayer. The final score was: A&M 50, Baylor 0.

Much heartened, the team followed the same prayer routine before the next game and beat SMU 48 to 0. And the following four games resulted in resounding victories for the Aggies.

Came the big Thanksgiving Day game against the University of Texas Longhorns. The Aggie coach gathered his players together and exhorted them to pray harder and longer than ever before. But the Aggies lost 99 to 0.

After the players had cleared the field, the spectators had left the stands and the clean-up crews were sweeping up the debris, the Aggie coach bowed his head and humbly beseeched his Maker: "Why, oh Lord," he cried, "Why did you let us down this time?"

Black storm clouds gathered in the sky; a streak of lightning flashed; a loud clap of thunder crashed; and a deep, solemn voice boomed, "Hook 'em, Horns."

The Aggie was bragging about his 60-year old father who had just taken top honors at the Huntsville prison rodeo.

"Shucks," said the University of Texas freshman, "my grandpaw is tougher than your old man. He's 85 and signed up last week to play end for a pro football team."

"Golly," exclaimed the Aggie, "I'd shore like to meet your grandpaw."

"Well, you can't right now. He's down home acting as best man at my great-grandpaw's wedding. He's 110."

"You've really got an amazing family," said the Aggie. "Your grandpaw's a football player at 85, and now your great-grandpaw wants to get married at 110."

"Hell, Aggie, you got that all wrong. Great grandpaw don't **want** to get married. He **has** to!"

One morning during a program experiment, an Aggie and a monkey were strapped in a rocket and launched from Cape Kennedy. The monkey had been trained to put on a set of earphones and follow verbal instructions from the Cape whenever a red light flashed on. The Aggie was told to put on his set of earphones and follow verbal instructions from the Cape whenever a green light flashed on.

At intervals all during the day while the rocket was in orbit the red light flashed and the monkey put on the earphones and, following instructions, pulled levers, twisted dials and executed a number of maneuvers in the ship. The Aggie was becoming more disgusted by the minute. Finally, late in the afternoon, the green light flashed. He eagerly picked up the earphones, placed them on his head and heard a voice from the Cape say, "Feed the monkey."

The medical school professor sent his students out to each purchase one pound of male brain matter for study. A group who arrived at the local medical supply house was given the prices:

Ph.D. Brains............................$ 37.50 per pound
Phi Beta Kappa Brains........................$ 32.50 per pound
Straight A Brains ....$ 25.00 per pound
Aggie Brains..$150.00 per pound

One young student questioned the price of Aggie brains noting, "I never thought they were that valuable."

The proprietor asked, "Have you ever thought how many Aggies it takes to make a pound of brains?"

QUESTION: Why does it take three Aggies to change a light bulb?
ANSWER: One to put the bulb in the socket and two to turn the ladder.

QUESTION: Why does it take five Aggies to pop popcorn?
ANSWER: One to hold the popper and four to shake the stove.

Three "X"s on a legal document can only mean one thing.
   Some Aggie found two classmates to go on his note at the bank.

Do you know why the Aggie grad lost his job as an elevator operator?
He couldn't learn the route!

16

Why are Aggies round shouldered and flat headed?

When you ask them a question . . .

When you tell them the answer . . .

QUESTION: Why does it take 2,368 Aggies to paint a house?
ANSWER: One to hold the brush while the rest turn the house.

QUESTION: What do you get when you cross an Aggie with a chimp?
ANSWER: A retarded monkey!

An Aggie had gone to see the doctor, who, after examining him told him to be careful about what he ate, in fact, not to eat at all until he got an appetite. Meeting the Aggie a few days later, the doctor asked how he felt.

"Oh, I feel fine now," the Aggie replied. "I waited one day, and I got no appetite; waited two days, no appetite; waited three days and still no appetite. I got so durn hungry I ate anyway."

The definition of gross ignorance is quickly given as 144 Aggies.

QUESTION: Do you know why it takes four Aggies to pull off a kidnapping?
ANSWER: One to carry the victim and three to write the ransom note.

A&M finally found a way to squash a rumor that had been circulating freely in academic circles.

The solution was to add two years to the engineering curriculum. One year to be devoted to geology and the other to anatomy.

That way no one could claim that Aggie engineers couldn't tell their rears from a hole in the ground.

Then there was the Aggie who thought "vice versa" meant dirty poems.

They say that the reason they limit A&M graduate engineers to five-minute coffee breaks at electronic plants is that longer intervals require extensive retraining.

How does an Aggie fan himself?

There was the Aggie walking down the street who saw a sign that read, "WET CEMENT," so he did.

The Aggie who was regarded as a social climber because he married a baboon.

"Young man," said the woman to an Aggie seated next to her on the jet flight, "Smoking makes me sick."

"Well, lady," said the Aggie blowing smoke rings. "If I were you I'd give it up."

The Aggie who went back to the farm on vacation and told his father that he was in the air corps because they sure taught him to pilot high in Barn Maintenance 103.

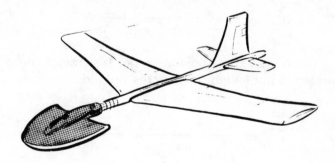

Did you hear about the Aggie who couldn't spell? It cost him $10 to spend the night in a warehouse.

Then there was the Aggie who threw himself on the floor and missed!

BARTENDER: What do you think of the moon shot?
AGGIE: Sounds good. I'll try one.

A fellow carrying two chickens in a sack met an Aggie. "If you can tell me how many chickens are in this sack, I'll give you both of them," he offered. "Five?" the Aggie replied.

Then there was the Aggie who got his tractor hung in reverse and unplowed three acres of land.

Two Aggies went hunting. They discovered some tracks, which they followed for quite some time. Then calamity struck! A train ran over them.

What goes around draped in a white sheet riding a pig?
Lawrence of A&M.

As four Aggies were going down the road they came to a high, solid brick wall. Wondering what was behind it, three of the Aggies boosted the fourth so he could look over it.

"Looks like a nudist camp," he exclaimed.

"Men or women?" his companions wanted to know.

"Can't tell," he answered. "They don't have any clothes on."

Did you hear about the flamingo that moved into a new home and put an Aggie in the front yard?

There was an Aggie who had stomach trouble and finally went to a doctor, who gave him a prescription. In two days the Aggie felt great and thanked the doctor profusely. The doctor told him he was glad he could help him, and added, "Frankly, I'm surprised you came to me." "Why?" asked the Aggie. "Because I'm a Teasipper," replied the doctor. "Oh, I don't mind Teasippers," said the Aggie, "it's those Baylor grads I can't stand. They're all either football players or fast women." Really!," said the affronted doctor, "I'll have you know my wife is a Baylor ex." "Sure 'nuff?" exclaimed the Aggie, "What position did she play?"

A Texas Tech student went into the men's furnishings department of a department store and asked for seven pairs of underwear. The clerk asked him why he wanted seven pairs. "For Monday, Tuesday, Wednesday, Thursday, Friday, Saturday and Sunday," the student replied. The next day a Baylor student asked the clerk for seven pairs of underwear, also for Monday, Tuesday, Wednesday, Thursday, Friday, Saturday and Sunday. Later, an Aggie asked the clerk for twelve pairs, and when the clerk asked what they were for, he answered, "January, February, March, April, May, June, July, August, September, October, November and December."

They had to close the library at A&M, because somebody stole the book. They opened the library at A&M, but had to close it again, because the guy who returned the book had colored it.

Five Aggies were trying to measure a telephone pole. One was on the bottom and the others were on his shoulders with yardsticks. A friend came by and suggested that since the pole was not tight in the ground, that they lay it down and measure it. The Aggie on the top said, "We don't want to know how long it is . . . we want to know how tall it is."

The Aggie ex, who was a traveling salesman, came home to Dallas unexpectedly during the middle of the week. The telephone rang late that night, and a man's voice at the other end asked, "Is the coast clear?" "How should I know," answered the Aggie. "That's 300 miles from here."

Did you hear about the Aggie who smelled bad under his left arm? He'd been using Right Guard.

An Aggie walked up to a group of scientists who were discussing algebra, calculus, geometry and trig. After listening politely for a while, he asked, "What do you fellows think about long division?"

_____

The Aggie in the pizza parlor, when asked by the waiter if he wanted his pie cut in six or eight pieces, replied, "Six. Don't believe I can eat eight."

_____

Preacher: "Do you want to go to heaven?"
   Aggie: "No, sir."
   Preacher: "Of course you want to go to heaven when you die."
   Aggie: "Oh sure, when I die. I thought you were getting up a crowd to go now."

_____

The Aggie was asked, "If you found a wallet with $1 million in it, would you give it back?"
   After some deliberation he replied, "If I thought they were poor people, I definitely would."

Three college students, one from A&M, one from SMU and one from the U. of Texas applied for a job at a farm. The farmer had only one opening, and said he'd employ the one who could stay in the pig sty longest. After one hour the Mustang came out of the sty, gasping, and fainted. After two hours the Teasipper crawled out on his hands and knees and collapsed. Three hours later, the pigs came out.

The Aggie was standing in the entrance of the Statler-Hilton Hotel lobby without a stitch of clothes on, when the policeman grabbed his arm and said, "Let's get something to cover you and go to the station." "Wait, officer, I'm an Aggie, and . . ." "I don't care if you are an Aggie, you can't stand here naked," the policeman interrupted. "But let me explain," pleaded the Aggie. "I'm waiting for my girl friend. We were up in the room and she said, let's get undressed and go to town.' I guess I beat her down."

First Aggie: I hear there's a new case of malaria in the dorm.

Second Aggie: Good! I'm getting awfully tired of Fresca.

"Why did they put this depot so far from town?" the traveling salesman asked an Aggie at a rural railroad station. "Well, stranger," said the Aggie, "I'm not sure, but I guess they wanted it as close to the tracks as possible."

A Texas Aggie moved to Oklahoma and raised the I.Q. level of both states.

Do you know what the city does when an Aggie fails to pay his garbage assessment? They stop the delivery.

A big, husky Aggie found work with a logging crew for the summer. The first week he sawed eight cords of wood a day with a hand saw. The foreman was so pleased, he issued him a power saw.

The following week the Aggie was still sawing eight cords of wood a day. The foreman ordered him to report to his office and bring the power saw with him.

In his office, the foreman said, "We gave you a power saw. Why haven't you increased your output?"

"I don't know," replied the Aggie, "I'm working harder than ever."

The foreman pulled the switch on the power saw, and the noise of the motor filled the room.

"What's that?" asked the Aggie.

An Aggie went hunting, and when he was deep into a forest he came upon a nude girl. "Are you game?" he asked. "Yes," was her reply. So he shot her.

Why did the Aggie cook his coffee in the bathtub?

Because the directions on the can said, "Boil it by the pot."

"What do you think of LSD?" the visitor asked the Aggie. "Well, I think he is the greatest President we ever had."

Two Aggie astronauts had been orbiting in space for 24 hours. One was outside the spacecraft taking pictures. When he got through with the assisnment, he found that the hatch door was closed, so he knocked on it. The Aggie inside called out, "Who is it?"

Preacher: "What must we do before God forgives us?"
    Aggie: "First we gotta sin."

An Aggie joined a paratrooper unit and the jump instructor showed the class how to pull the rip cord. "Yell 'Geronimo!' and pull the rip cord," he told them. "If the parachute doesn't open, flap your arms like you're flying," he added.

The Aggie jumped and frantically knocked on the door of the plane, yelling, "What was that Indian's name, again?"

Do you know how an Aggie does his "nine" multiplication tables?

He can remember that 9x1 is 9
Then, he writes down . . .
9 x 2
9 x 3
9 x 4
9 x 5
9 x 6
9 x 7
9 x 8
9 x 9

Then, he puts a progressive number from top to bottom beside each one . . .
9 x 2 is 1
9 x 3   2
9 x 4   3
9 x 5   4
9 x 6   5
9 x 7   6
9 x 8   7
9 x 9   8

Then, he goes back and adds a progressive number from bottom to top . . .
9 x 2 is 18
9 x 3   27
9 x 4   36
9 x 5   45
9 x 6   54
9 x 7   63
9 x 8   72
9 x 9   81

Then there was the Aggie whose breath was so bad they tipped him over on Halloween.

An Aggie science major was invited to attend a symposium conducted by the nation's most notable space scientists. He listened attentively as the speaker read papers on various projects to send astronauts to the moon, to Mars, to Venus, etc. During the round-table discussion that followed, the Aggie said, "Gentlemen, I've listened with interest to your plans, however, we're planning an even greater project. We plan to send a rocket to the sun." "But that's absurd," the scientists told him. "You can't do that. The heat will be so intense it will melt the rocket before it can land." The Aggie replied, "Ah, we've got that licked! We're going at night."

A bunch of farmers were discussing the veracity of an A&M graduate who had bought a farm in the area.

His nearest neighbor was asked his opinion. "What do you think about it? Would you call that Aggie a big liar?"

"Now, now, boys," he replied, "I wouldn't go that far and call him a liar exactly, but I do know this much — when feedin' time comes, in order to get any response from his hogs, he has to get someone else to call 'em for him."

Two Aggies traveling around the world, chanced to meet on a street in Paris. "Would you believe it," said one, 'I've been here four days and I still haven't been to the Louvre." "Neither have I," the other replied. "It must be the water."

The Aggie set up a barber service in his dorm to help finance his education. He worked hard cutting the hair of his first customer, his room mate. He snipped and snipped and finally finished with a flourish of the scissors. He held a mirror in back of his room mate's head and asked, "Is that all right?"

"Almost," was the reply, "Just a little longer in back, please.

A University of Texas ex bought an outhouse and rented the basement to an Aggie ex.

A lady called a painter to estimate painting the interior of her home. After touring each room and hearing her color preferences, he leaned out of the window and hollered, "Green side up" to several helpers in the yard.

This went on, room after room. When they were finished, she took him to task about not paying attention to her color instructions, and calling, "green side up" to his helpers outside.

"Oh, I was paying attention, mam. My helpers out there are Aggies and they're laying grass sod next door. I was just making sure that they were laying the sod properly," the painter explained.

Noting the filthy condition of the freshman's socks, the Aggie football coach admonished him. "You must put on a clean pair of socks every day before we go out for practice," he commanded. By Friday, the freshman couldn't get his shoes on.

On the menu of an Austin restaurant: "SPECIAL AGGIE SANDWICH. Half Tongue and Half Chicken."

First Man: Did you hear about the Aggie who could count to ten?
Second Man: No.
First Man: would you believe five?

"Open Other End" is stamped on the bottom of all Dr.
Pepper bottles made in College Station.

Then there was the Aggie who called Braniff Flight Information and asked the clerk, "How long does it take to fly to Oklahoma City?" "Just a minute, sir," replied the clerk. "Thank you," said the Aggie and hung up.

When the Aggie heard that **95** percent of automobile accidents happen within five miles of home, he moved.

INTERVIEWER: How do you spell Mississippi?
AGGIE: Do you want the river or the state?

The Aggie was filling out the physical education question-
aire form and came to the question, "Have your eyes ever
been checked?" "No," he wrote, "They've always been
blue."

The doctor told the Aggie who came to him for a physical check-up to strip to the waist.
So the Aggie removed his trousers.

Do you know how to tell a happy motorcycling Aggie? By the bugs in his teeth.

Prof: You missed class yesterday, didn't you?
Aggie: No, sir, not a bit.

The sound of the crash was shattering and the wreckage scattered all over the place when the Aggie, racing to beat the train to the crossing, hit the 23rd car.

"Son," said the Aggie's mother, "run across the street and see how old Mrs. Brown is this morning."
A few minutes later he returned. "Maw," he reported, "Mrs. Brown says it's none of your business how old she is."

Did you hear about the Aggie who stayed up all night studying for his urine test?

The Aggies' arms were loaded with rolls of toilet paper.
"Where are you going?" his friend asked.
"To an all-night crap game," replied the Aggie.

Two Aggies were enjoying a wonderful afternoon in a rowboat. The weather was perfect; the fish were biting; everything was fine, until a motorboat raced by and caused the rowboat to ship water.

"Let's bail," suggested one of the Aggies.

"No, that's inefficient," said the other. "Let's just bore a hole in the bottom of the boat and let the water drain out by itself."

So they drilled the hole, and more water rushed in. They then figured that a second hole was needed so that the water coming in through the first opening could find a place through which it could flow back into the lake.

Sit down in front," the spectators at the prize fight shouted to the Aggie who was obstructing their view. "I can't" the Aggie hollered back, "I don't bend that way."

There's a rumor out that Baylor and Texas A&M are going to merge, and the students will be known as "Baggies."

Do you know what Aggies do with birth control pills?
They feed them to storks.

The police officer investigating a burning house discovered an Aggie inside drinking a bottle of wine. "Did you set this house on fire," asked the officer.

"Hell, no," the Aggie replied. "It was on fire when I came in."

Did you hear about the Aggie who thought Minnie Pearl was a short beer?

Mechanic: I've got six torsion arms.
Aggie: Maybe you'd better see a doctor.

Customer: I want some sealing wax.
Aggie Salesman: You must be kidding. Who'd want to wax a ceiling.

Definition of a dope ring:—ten Aggies standing in a circle.

How to keep an Aggie busy.
(over)

How to keep an Aggie busy.
(over)

T-sipper: May I join you?
  Aggie: Why, am I coming apart?

_____

There was the Aggie who crossed a cow with an octopus to get a do-it-yourself milker.

Did you hear about the Aggie who thought Shirley Temple was a synagogue?

_____

His brother Aggie thought alabaster was an illegitimate Mohammedan.

_____

When the Aggie's wife had triplets, he grabbed a double-barrelled shotgun and rushed out to kill the other two guys.

_____

Cross an Aggie with an ape and you get a hairy ape or a stupid county agent.

_____

An Aggie visited a big city for the first time. He was trying to cross Main St. one evening. Because the light was red, he waited. Then a green sign lit up. It read, "WALK," so he got out of his car.

Too bad about the Aggie who lost the Indianapolis 500. He made five stops — three to re-fuel and two to ask directions.

"Do you file your fingernails?" the T-sipper asked. "No, I just throw them away," the Aggie replied.

The Aggie's shirt was soaking wet when he picked up his date. "Why is your shirt so wet?" she asked. Replied the Aggie, "Well, the label inside says, wash and wear."

T-sipper: I heard about a guy who gets involved in a car accident 12 times a week.
  Aggie: Why doen't he sell his car?

The Aggie was delivering newspapers when his bicycle skidded and he hit the milk bottles on the porch. "Gosh," he exclaimed, "I've run into a cow's nest!"

Aggies think an igloo is a substance that keeps two igs together.

QUESTION: Do you know why dalmatians ride on the Aggie firetrucks?
  ANSWER: To find the hydrants.

T-sipper: Sam Smith has E.S.P.
  Aggie: Yes, he catches anything that comes along.

Did you hear about the Aggie who ran out of ice cubes and couldn't make any more because he lost the recipe?

An Aggie got a summer job selling outhouses to farmers. He sold one-holers for $150 and two-holers for $200 and, during the course of the summer, sold several hundred . . . because he guaranteed that they wouldn't stink. Before school started again in the fall, he decided to call on all his customers to be sure they were satisfied with the product. But, upon calling on the first farmer, he was astounded to see him boiling mad.

"Say, young man," the farmer said, "didn't you guarantee my outhouse wouldn't smell?" The Aggie agreed he had done so. But, before refunding the farmer his money, the Aggie said he wanted to take a look to see if he could find the trouble. A few minutes later, the Aggie returned. "No wonder," the Aggie exclaimed. "Look what you've gone and done in there!"

The Aggie filled out the application for employment and in the blank labelled "Church Preference" he wrote "Red Brick."

Did you hear about the Aggie who disappeared? Somebody gave him an enema and a haircut.

Did you hear about the Japanese Aggie who on December 7, 1941, attacked Pearl Bailey?

———————————

He was a friend of the Aggie kamakazi pilot with 1200 missions.

———————————

"Doctor, I've been married three times, yet I'm still a virgin," the attractive young woman complained.

"How did that happen?" asked the doctor.

"Well, my first husband was an optometrist and just wanted to look. My second husband was a chiropractor and just wanted to feel. My third husband was an Aggie and he said 'Wait till next year!' "

Did you hear about the Aggie's dog that got run over by a parked car?

Asked what he thought of the Civil Rights bill, an Aggie replied, "Well, if we owe it, we ought to pay it."

The Aggie read the surgeon general's report which said that studies proved tar and nicotine caused cancer in mice, so he put his cigarettes up high where the mice couldn't get at them.

An Aggie and his friend were walking along a street in Dallas looking for a place to eat. They stopped in front of a clean looking restaurant and read the sign which said, "Luncheon, 11 to 2, $1.50."

"Let's go in and eat here," said the Aggie. "It ain't such a bad bargain—three hours of steady eatin' for only $1.50."

The best thing to come out of College Station is Highway 6.

———————

Texas A&M doesn't like to play Texas Tech, because the Tech players have TT on their sweatshirts.

Most Aggies think Johnny Cash is a pay toilet.

An Aggie courting his girl friend gazed into her eyes and said, "I love you," as he caressed her tummy. "Lower, lower," she murmured." "I love you," said the Aggie in tones an octave lower.

Did you hear about the Aggie who looked into a lumber yard for the draft board?

"**G**uess what this is," said the T-sipper, holding his nose and flapping his coattails. "I give up," replied his companion. "It's a vulture flying over a dead Aggie."

Aggie: What subjects do you teach the children at this school?

Principal: Reading, writing, geography, spelling and trigonometry.

Aggie: Well, give my boy some trigonometry. He's the worst shot in our county.

When the garbage collectors' strike was going on in New York City, a bunch of Aggies there got together and held a big luau.

And there was the Aggie who drank so much Fresca he snowed in his pants.

There was an Aggie who was so big that when he died they couldn't find a coffin large enough. So they gave him an enema and put him in a shoebox.

The Aggie met a lovely girl from Houston at a corps dance, danced almost every dance with her, and, when the evening was over, asked if he might see her on his next trip to Houston. "Yes," she replied. So he got out his notebook and asked, "What's your phone number?" "CApitol 2-1849," she said. There was a long pause, and the Aggie asked, "How do you make a capital 2?"

It took the Aggie a whole day to wash three basement windows. It took six hours to dig the hole to put the ladder in.

Do you know what they call a thousand Aggie paratroopers?
Air pollution.

Then there was the Aggie who bought a pair of water skis and then looked for a lake with a hill in it.

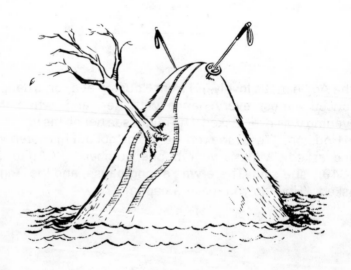

A puzzle manufacturer has come out with a one-piece jigsaw puzzle for Aggies.

T-sipper: What do you think about the international crisis?
   Aggie: It's unquestionably the best model they ever made.

An Aggie locked his car keys in his convertible. He called a locksmith, who told him he was too busy to come. "Please come," pleaded the Aggie. "My key's locked up in the car, it's starting to rain, and the top's down.

Did you hear about the Aggies who were throwing firecrackers at the T-sippers?

Well, the T-sippers lit them and threw them back at the Aggies.

Did you hear about the Aggie who underwent a heart transplant operation? The heart rejected the body.

It was an Aggie who completed the first successful transplant of a hernia.

Did you hear about the Aggie who went to the butcher shop and asked for five karate chops?

An Aggie sent off for his family tree and got back a bunch of bananas.

Did you hear about the Aggie who sold his typewriter because it missed two periods and he thought it was pregnant?

QUESTION: Why do so many Aggies wear turtle necks?
ANSWER: To hide the flea collars.

The Aggie with kidney trouble is easy to spot because of his rusty zipper and yellow tennis shoes.

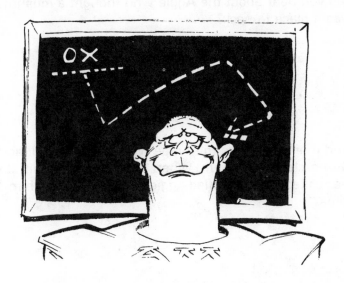

Even on basic plays, the great Aggie football prospect proved to be so stupid, the coach decided to give him individual help after practice every day.

"I'm going to diagram plays so you'll know exactly what you are supposed to do each time," the coach told the boy as he stood in front of a blackboard. "Now the X's I'm going to draw on the board will be us: the O's will be the other team."

The skull practices continued three days, then on the fourth day the boy didn't show up. The coach sought him out and asked why.

"It's all them X's and O's." the boy explained. "I just can't keep it straight in my head who is us and who is them!"

Did you hear about the Aggie who thought a mushroom was a place to neck?

And then there was the Aggie who was having difficulty with a chemistry exam. When a definition of "nitrates" was called for, the baffled Aggie wrote: "Cheaper than day rates."

"Will you help me straighten up the house?" the Aggie's wife asked him.

"Why?" replied the Aggie, "Is it tilted?"

Did you hear about the two Aggies who were shooting craps?

They blew a hole in the toilet.

Did you hear about the Aggie who was so narrow minded a fly could speck in both eyes at one time?

An Aggie went to a drugstore and asked the clerk for a package of condoms. The clerk said, "They are packaged three for $1." The Aggie handed him a dollar bill, and the clerk said, "That will be $1.05." "What's the five cents for?" asked the Aggie. "Tax," the clerk replied. "Why?" the Aggie said, "I thought you just rolled 'em on."

Then there was the Aggie who thought logarithm was a birth control method for lumbermen.

Two Aggies who were members of the highway patrol caught a motorist speeding on the outskirts of Waxahachie. One of the Aggies started to make out the ticket, and asked the other, "How do you spell Waxahachie?" "Gosh, I don't know," the other Aggie replied. "Let's let him go and catch up with him at Waco."

An inebriated Aggie fell off a 10-story building. A policeman rushed up to him. "What happened?" the officer inquired. Replied the Aggie: "Don't know, officer, just got here myself."

Did you hear about the Aggie who was so dumb he thought a bar stool was something Davy Crockett stepped in.

Did you hear about the Aggie who worked at General Dynamics and thought tail assembly was the company picnic?

Then there was the Aggie who invested heavily in frozen radio dinners.

There was an Aggie who read a big city newspaper for the first time. As he read the obituary page, he scratched his head and muttered, "That's mighty strange." The next day he read the newspaper and when he finished reading the obituary section, he exclaimed. "Well I'll be darned, it happened again." The next day he read the newspaper and the obituary page and commented, "It's amazing. The folks here die alphabetically!"

Did you hear about the Aggie who thought bacteria was the rear entrance to a cafe?

A well plastered Aggie was driving along merrily the wrong way down a one-way street, until stopped by a patrolman.

"Didn't you see the arrows?" asked the cop.

"The arrows?" answered the inebriated Aggie. "I didn't even see the Indians."

The Aggie had filled out a job application blank and later was interviewed by the personnel manager.

Noting that the applicant had omitted the year of his birth, the personnel manager said: "I see that your birthday is August 16. May I ask what year?"

"Every year," the Aggie replied.

Did you hear about the Aggie who said he'd give his right arm to be ambidextrous?

———————————

Did you hear about the Aggie who went to a seance, and no one would hold his hand?

———————————

Two Aggies drove to a lumberyard. One stayed in the car, while the other went inside to buy some lumber.

"I want to order some 4 x 2's," he told the clerk.

"Don't you mean 2 x 4's?" the clerk asked.

"Wait a minute, I'll check with my partner," the Aggie said.

After checking with his friend, he returned and said, "Yes, 2 x 4's will be okay."

"How long do you want them?" the clerk asked.

"Wait, I'll check with my partner," the Aggie said.

In a few minutes the Aggie returned and said, "We'll want them a long time. We're going to build a garage."

———————————

Did you hear about the Aggie quarterback who called for a fair catch when his center snapped the ball?

Do you know why Aggies' dogs have flat noses?
From chasing parked cars.

Did you hear about the Aggie who jumped out of bed and broke one of his socks?

"Take these pills two days running, then skip a day," the doctor told the Aggie. "Follow this routine for two weeks, then report back to me."

At the end of one week, the Aggie went back to the doctor. "I'm tired, doctor," he complained. "That skipping wore me out."

T-SIPPER: I broke my arm in three places:
  AGGIE: You ought to stay out of those places.

Then there was an Aggie who thought Jonathan Winters was an air conditioned outhouse.

Did you hear about the Aggie who was so dumb he thought a half horse trailer was a trailer for two quarter horse?

Did you hear about the Aggie skier with the frostbitten fanny? He couldn't figure how to get his pants on over the skis.

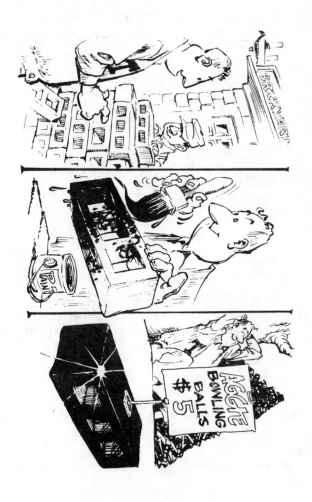

Before his first plane ride an Aggie was told that chewing gum would keep his ears from popping during the flight. After finally landing he turned to his seat companion and said, "The chewing gum works fine, but how do I get it out of my ears?"

A small Texas town purchased a new fire truck. The next time the councilmen met they discussed how to dispose of the old one.

The Aggie councilman suggested they keep it and use it for false alarms.

Do you know what you get when you cross an Aggie with a roadrunner.

Well, I'm not really sure, but if you can ever catch it, you can be sure it will be the ugliest creature in brown boots.

Did you hear about the Aggie who thought "Peter Pan" was something to put under the bed?

Two Aggies were driving home from work when one of them said, "Let's stop and get a beer at this great new place I found. The bar stools are numbered, and if your number is called, you can go upstairs for free sex." "Have you ever won," the other Aggie asked. "No," replied the first Aggie, "but my wife won twice last week."

Disgusted with the players during practice, the Aggie coach called them together and laid down the law. "Look, men, I'm convinced that before we can make any further progress, we must go back to the fundamentals." He reached over and picked up a ball.

"Now this," he said, holding it up, "is a football. It . . ."

At this point a tackle interrupted: "Please, coach, no so fast!"

Did you hear about the Aggie who lost his girl friend?
He forgot where he laid her.

QUESTION: What is this?

T-Sipper: What do you think of marijuana?
  Aggie: It's one of the worst border towns I've ever seen.

ANSWER: Two Aggies, walking abreast.

Two Aggies were watching a trombone player perform. One turned to the other and said, "I'll bet you $10 that guy isn't swallowing that thing."

The Aggie came in to work at 11 o'clock and the boss shouted, "You should have been here two hours ago!" The Aggie said, "Why? What happened then?"

Five Southwest Conference schools are installing synthetic football turf at a cost of $300,000, but the Aggies are paying $400,000. Reason: They're including an underground sprinkler system.

An Aggie spent a holiday in New Mexico with the Indians who told him the Legend of the Maidens. According to this legend, there are beautiful Indian maidens who live in large caves and crevices, they said. "If you hear them call, 'woo, woo,' take off your clothes quickly and enter the cave. They will show you a fabulous time."

Several days later, the headlines in the local newspaper read, "Body of Naked Aggie Found in Tunnel, Run over by Train."

In Las Vegas, an Aggie was running up and down putting dimes in parking meters. A curious bystander asked, "What are you doing?" The Aggie replied, "I love this outdoor gambling."

The T-Sipper was jumping up and down on a manhole cover, chanting, "54, 54, 54."

An Aggie came by and demanded to know what it was all about. The T-Sipper told him to try it himself. As the Aggie jumped up and down, the T-Sipper released a lever. The manhole cover gave way and the Aggie disappeared.

The T-Sipper then secured the cover again, and began to jump up and down on it chanting, "55, 55, 55, 55."

A T-Sipper was piloting a plane load of Aggies from Little Rock to College Station. Bad weather forced them to circle over Bryan. As the fog continued, they kept circling for almost an hour. Finally, the pilot announced over the p.a. system, "I have bad news and good news. The bad news is that we are running of gas. The good news is, I'm parachuting down to get help."

T-Sipper: Why don't you get an encyclopedia?
Aggie: It's too much work pumping up hills.

Did you hear about the Aggie who thought Nixon was one of Santa's reindeer?

There were two Aggies who went horseback riding every day, but couldn't tell the horses apart. One docked his horse's tail, but one day the horse with the long tail got it caught in a gate, so the two tails were the same length. One Aggie then put a notch in his horse's ear, but the other horse notched his ear on a wire fence. Finally, the two Aggies thought of measuring the horses, and discovered the white horse was two inches taller than the black horse.

An Aggie was taken to play golf for the first time. When he was told to tee off, he ran to the woods.

T-Sipper: What do you think of the Vietnam position.
    Aggie: My wife and I tried it, but it hurt her back.

Did you hear about the Aggie who thought asphalt was rectum trouble?

Do you know what April 1 is?
    Aggie Day.

An Aggie was sitting in his brand new car when three tough-looking hippies came up. "Get out of your car," said one of the hippies. "Now stand inside this circle and if you get out of it we'll break your neck."

The Aggie got inside the circle and the hippies started to demolish his new car. While his car was being mutilated, the Aggie roared with laughter.

"What are you laughing at?" screamed the hippie.

"Ha, ha," laughed the Aggie, "The joke's on you. I jumped out of this circle three times while you weren't looking!"

And then there's the Aggie who is so dumb he thinks Gatorade is welfare for crocodiles.

Two Aggies were hunting and became lost. One said to the other, "Do you know where we are?" "No," was the reply.

"I guess we're lost," said the first Aggie. "Why don't we shoot three shots in the air. That's the distress signal."

"Okay," said the second Aggie. "Shoot."

So the first Aggie shot three times. They waited and nothing happened. They walked about a mile, then the second Aggie said, "Nothing's happened. Shoot three more times." The first Aggie did so. Nothing happened. They walked a little farther. Then the second Aggie said, "Shoot again." "Can't," said the first Aggie. "Why?" "Ran out of arrows."

T-Sipper: I was born under Taurus, the Bull.
   Aggie: Boy, I'll bet he was surprised!

T-Sipper: Do you need glasses?
  Aggie: Only when I drink.

Then there was the Aggie who was so ugly, it took Polaroid an hour to develop his picture.

A city-bred Aggie got so worried about the ecology situation that he gave up his job in the city and moved to a farm. He was so concerned, that he decided he wouldn't use tractors or any other equipment that might add to pollution problems. So he contacted the owner of the farm next to his and asked him if he had any horse eggs for sale, as he planned to do the plowing with horses. "No," his neighbor replied, "I'm fresh out of horse eggs, but you try the next farmer down the road. I think he might have a few left."

When the Aggie left, the farmer called the next farmer down the road and clued him in. The second farmer immediately painted two watermelons brown. When the Aggie arrived on his quest, the farmer said, "You're lucky, I just have two horse eggs left." "How much are they?" asked the Aggie. The farmer replied, "$75 each." "Well, that seems a mighty high price," the Aggie said. The farmer explained that horses were becoming increasingly in demand and scarce, so the Aggie bought the two "eggs."

On his way home, he dropped one of the "eggs" in a ravine. It broke and a jackrabbit jumped out of the ravine. "Well," the Aggie said to himself. "It was a good egg all right, but the horse would have been too fast to hitch up to a plow, anyway!"

"I have a friend who is a great scuba enthusiast. He is president of the state scuba club and spends all his spare time scuba diving," the T-Sipper said.

"But," asked the Aggie, "what does he do with all those scubas?"

The toughest thing in College Station for an Aggie is riding shot gun on a garbage truck.

Do you know what an Aggie thinks Spade Cooley is?
  A castrated Chinaman.

An Aggie was asked, "What do you think of the Indianapolis 500?"
  "They're all innocent," he replied.

T-Sipper: Do you have any pornography?
  Aggie: No. I don't even have a pornograph.

The county agent who was visiting a farmer noticed a television antenna on the outhouse, and asked the farmer why it was there.

"We installed indoor plumbing, and rented the outhouse to a University of Texas student," explained the farmer.

"He must be a pretty dumb guy to live there," the county agent commented.

"Heck, he's not so dumb," the farmer replied. "He sublet the basement to an Aggie."

An Aggie married a Greek girl, and in due course they had a baby boy. It is the Greek custom to give the child a name reflecting the heritage of both parents. So they named the baby, Zorba, the Dumb Ass.

Two Aggies were traveling on a jet airliner when the pilot informed the passengers that they have lost one engine, but there is no cause for alarm, as they have plenty of power left, but the flight will only be a little late. Later another engine went out, and the pilot repeated the message. Later the third engine went out and the pilot delivered the same story. Then the first Aggie said to the second Aggie, "You know, if that last engine goes out, we may be up here all night."

It's easy to tell where an Aggie lives. He is the only one in the neighborhood who has crabgrass **inside** the house.

Two Aggies were sitting in a tavern drinking beer. One of them remarked, "Do you think Ali MacGraw is her real name?" The other Aggie, mulling over the question, sipped his beer a few times and matter-of-factly replied, "Do I think whose real name is Ali MacGraw?"

An Aggie tried out for pro football. The coach, interviewing him on the practice field, asked what position he hoped to play. "Quarterback," answered the Aggie. The coach handed him a football and said, "Do you think you can pass this ball?" "Heck yes, if I can swallow it," the Aggie replied.

Definition of a galloping gourmet: an Aggie running after a garbage truck.

Did you hear about the Aggie who was such a poor reader he belonged to the Page of the Month Club.

A Baylor grad, a Texas U. grad and an Aggie were in Mexico, got drunk and killed a Mexican. All three went to jail and were sentenced to the electric chair. First, they sat the Baylor grad down and asked him if he had any last words. He said he was a dentist and would care for everyone in the village for 25 years if they would let him go. They said they were sorry, but they had to carry out the execution. They pulled the switch and nothing happened.

The executioner said that by law, the Baylor grad was a free man, because the electric chair didn't work. Then the Texas U. grad sat down. The same question was asked. He said he was a medical graduate and would care for the villagers for 25 years in exchange for his freedom. Again, the answer was no. The switch was pulled and nothing happened. He got off free.

Then the Aggie sat down. When asked if he had any last words, the Aggie said that he was a graduate in electrical engineering from Texas A&M, and, he told the executioner, "if you'll put that little white wire in that hole, and the little red wire in that hole . . ."

Did you hear about the Aggie scientist who developed an artificial appendix?

Do you know why Aggies eat beans on Friday? So they can have a bubble bath on Saturday.

The Aggie had a bad breath problem and went to the doctor, who gave him a series of tests and told him to come back the following day for his diagnosis. When he returned the next day, the doctor told him: ''You have to do one of two things — either quit scratching your ass, or quit biting your fingernails.''

The Aggie was asked if he preferred red or white wine with dinner. "It doesn't make any difference," he said. "I'm color blind."

Did you hear about the Aggie who thought High Cholesterol was a religious holiday?

Texas A&M discontinued its driver education program. The mule died.

Two Aggies were preparing for a math exam. One asked the other, "How many degrees are there in a circle?" Answered the second Aggie after considerable thought, "How big is that circle?"

Did you hear about the Aggie who went to Zales to buy a tornado watch?

An Aggie was trying to light a match. He struck the first match. It didn't work; he threw it away. He struck the second match. That didn't work either and he threw it away. He struck the third one and it lit up. He blew it out and said, "That's a good one. I've got to save it."

The Aggie's gums shriveled up and his teeth started falling out, so he went to a dentist. After examining his mouth, the dentist said, "Your mouth is in terrible condition. Do you brush your teeth?" "Of course I do," the Aggie replied indignantly. "Every day." "Well, what do you brush them with?" the dentist asked. "I use Preparation H," said the Aggie.

T-SIPPER: Did you know that Mars and the Earth have the same sun?

AGGIE: No, I didn't even know they were married.

The Houston Astros had an Aggie catcher whose chief problem was he couldn't remember people — a distinctive handicap when it came to advising the pitcher what to throw to a batter. But the catcher didn't just fail to recognize the enemy. He had no idea as to the names of his teammates.

When this catcher's roommate of the previous year met him at training camp the next spring, the roomie chided him. "I bet you don't remember me," he challenged. "Of course I do," said the Aggie triumphantly, "You're Number 4."

T-SIPPER: Did you see the eclipse last night?

AGGIE: No, it was so dark I couldn't see a thing.

POLICE CAPTAIN: "He got away, did he? Didn't I tell you to cover all of the exits?"

AGGIE COP: "Yes, sir. I did, too. But I think he must have walked out through one of the entrances."

Do you know how to spoil an Aggie's party?
Flush the punch bowl.

An Aggie went to a paper company and ordered a roll of paper ½ inch wide and 50 feet long. "Why do you need paper that size," asked the paper salesman. "I'm moving, and need it to pack my clothesline," the Aggie replied.

Then there was the Aggie who thought a rebuttal was a fanny transplant.

The Aggie farmer was lifting hogs, one by one, up to his apple trees to graze on the apples. His T-Sipper friend asked him, "Doesn't that take a lot of time?" The Aggie replied, "What's time to a hog?"

Did you hear about the Aggie who phoned a camera store and asked if he could rent some flash bulbs?

T-SIPPER: Where was Joan of Arc burned?
   AGGIE: All over her body.

Did you hear about the Aggie who won a gold medal in the Olympics? He was so proud of it he had it bronzed.
He won the medal in the javelin-catching event.

FIRST AGGIE: Let's get us a couple of girls and go out and do the town.

SECOND AGGIE: Well, I don't know. I got a case of diarrhea.

FIRST AGGIE: Bring it along, we'll drink it.

An Aggie went into a bar and a good looking gal sat down next to him. He started to chat with her and after a while said, "How about our partying together tonight?" "Thank you for the invitation," she replied, "but I think it's only fair to tell you that I'm a lesbian." "Oh," replied the Aggie, "is that so? Well, how are things in Beirut?"

Did you hear about the rich Aggie whose girlfriend told him she liked hard rock — so he bought her the Petrified Forest?

There's one way to tell an Aggie's underwear from a T-Sipper's. Throw them both on a roof. The one that sticks is the Aggie's.

An Aggie, wearing a mask and carrying a gun, walked into a bank, went to a tellers window, slammed down a $20 bill and barked, "Give me all of your brown paper bags."

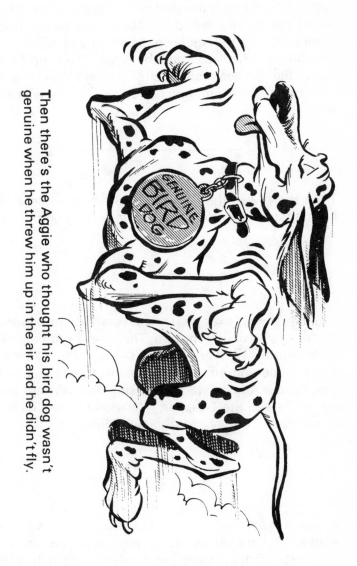

Then there's the Aggie who thought his bird dog wasn't genuine when he threw him up in the air and he didn't fly.

An Aggie went to the pet shop to complain about his canary that wouldn't sing. The owner said, "File the beak just a little bit, and the bird will sing. But if you file it too much the canary will die." About two weeks later the owner ran into the Aggie on the street and inquired about his canary. "He died," said the Aggie. "But, sir, I told you not to file the beak too much." "I didn't" said the Aggie, "but by the time I got him out of the vise, he was already dead."

———————————

Then there was the Aggie who got hurt while elephant hunting in Africa. He got a hernia setting up the decoys.

———————————

A University of Texas grad had several A&M grads and one Baylor grad working for him. The Baylor grad stood on a table with his right arm raised, saying, "I'm a light bulb." The T-Sipper, figuring he was insane, fired him. Later that day, all the Aggies started walking out. "Where are you going?" asked the T-Sipper. "You don't expect us to work in the dark!" one of the Aggies replied.

———————————

A Texas A&M engineering student was on an elevator with a number of other passengers. As the elevator moved up, he stared at the small fan slowly turning in the elevator ceiling. "I'm amazed that such a small fan can lift all these people," he remarked to the passengers.

Did you hear about the Aggie who became a millionaire?
He discovered a way to grow synthetic turf!

An Aggie introduced himself to a cute chick in a cocktail
lounge. After a while he asked her for a date. "I never date
Aggies," she told him. "How do you know I'm an Aggie,"
he asked. "You have B.O. and you're wearing your boots
on the wrong feet," she replied.

Do you know how an Aggie spells "farm?"
   E I E I O.

Did you hear about the Aggie who hijacked a 747? He demanded 250,000 parachutes and one dollar. His roommate hijacked a submarine, and demanded a million dollars and a parachute.

An Aggie and his friend were trading hair-raising experiences. "Then when a big truck was on my tail, I lost control of my car and headed straight for a brick wall,' the Aggie said. "What happened then?" asked his friend breathlessly. "My dime ran out," the Aggie replied.

Did you hear about the Aggie who thought Oral Sex was a course in marriage counseling at a university in Oklahoma?

An Aggie in a bait shop asked the clerk, "How much are the plastic worms?" "All you want for $1," the clerk told him. "Okay, I"ll take $2 worth," the Aggie said.

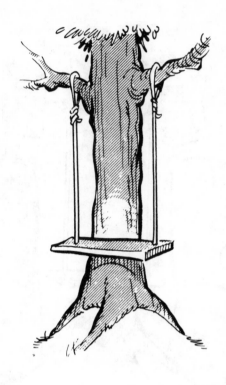

The first "Aggie Swing" before three famous Aggie Engineers tried it and revised it.

(over)

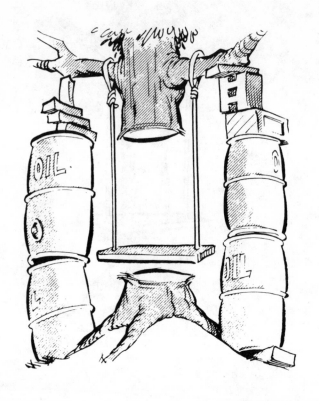

The revised Aggie Swing

An Aggie was painting his house one hot August day and was asked why he was wearing two jackets. "The directions on the can said to put on two coats," he answered.

Did you hear about the Aggie who thought penicillin was a cure for writer's cramp?

Three Aggies were close friends all of their lives. One died, and at his funeral his two friends viewed the body before the lid of the coffin was closed. "He sure looks good," said one. "Well, he ought to. He jogged five miles every day," said the other.

An Aggie, a S.M.U. student and a Texas Tech student were rapping about who they'd like to be cast off on a desert with. The S.M.U. student opted for Sophia Loren. The Texas Tech man chose Lisa Minnelli. The Aggie picked Virginia Pipeline. "Never heard of her," his companions protested. "Who is she?" "Why, she's just the greatest Italian gal of all, making the headlines in the newspaper," replied the Aggie. "See, here it is on page one:

FIVE DIE LAYING
VIRGINIA PIPELINE"

An Aggie bought a handsome Ford station wagon with walnut paneling and chrome stripes and railings on the outside. After it was delivered to his home he took a crowbar and started prying the wood panels and metal strips off of the car. After two hours hard work, he stood back and surveyed his work, and said disgustedly, "Hell, I think it looked better before I uncrated it."

Two Aggies bought a small pick-up truck and went into business selling watermelons. They bought watermelons in Sherman for $1.25 each, hauled them to Dallas and sold them for $1.25 each. After the first month, one partner totaled up the ledger and announced, "We haven't made a dime this month," His partner replied, "See, I told you we should have bought a bigger truck."

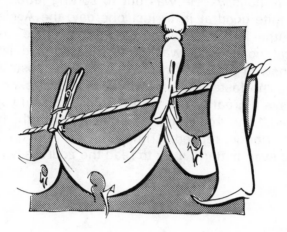

Do you know how you can tell you're in Aggieland?

By the toilet paper hanging out to dry on all the clotheslines.

What is dumb looking, ugly, and rings your doorbell once a month?

The Avon Aggie.

An Aggie asked the librarian for a good book to read.

"Do you want something light or do you prefer a heavier book?" asked the librarian.

"It really doesn't matter," the Aggie assured her. "I have my car outside."

The Aggie got a job in the post office during the Christmas holidays. He was put to sorting letters. And he got quite good at it. In just one day, the Aggie had become the fastest letter sorter in post office history. The local postmaster was quite pleased and let the Aggie know of his pleasure. "Son," said the postmaster. "you are the fastest letter sorter I have ever seen. You could have a great future with the post office if you are interested." The Aggie, too, was pleased with the praise and full of pride, replied, "Thank you, sir. Tomorrow I'll try to do even better. I'll try to read the addresses."

Did you hear about the Aggie who put snow tires on his car? The next day they melted.

Two Aggies were trying to get a mule into a barn, but the door was so low that the mule's ears would hit the top. They tried and tried to get him in, but couldn't. A T-Sipper came along and told them to pull the mule out, dig out a little in the doorway, and lead the mule on in. After a while, one Aggie said to the other, "That just shows you how dumb a T-Sipper is. Hell, it isn't his legs that are too long, it's his ears."

Do you know why Aggies save the ring tabs off of beer cans?

To use as combination class rings and pop-up nose pickers.

Did you know you can get the latest Aggie joke by dialing ESQUIRE on your telephone?

A Rice man thinks seated, a Texas man standing, a Baylor man pacing, and an Aggie afterward.

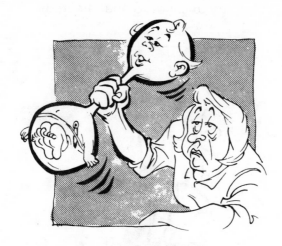

Aggie mothers are strong and square-shouldered from raising dumb-bells.

The Texas ex had an Aggie for a brother. The Texas ex was out of town when his wife had their first child, so the Aggie brother had to take her to the hospital. She gave birth to twins. According to County law, infants had to be named immediately after birth. So, the Aggie had to name the twins. He called his brother and told him he had named the girl twin, "Denise." "Why, that's really a very pretty name," said the Texas ex brother, "and what did you name the boy twin?" "De Nephew," replied the Aggie.

Be sure to watch the two-hour TV special tonight. An Aggie is going to try to count to one hundred.

The Aggie math student when asked how high he could count, counted to five on his hand. When asked if that was as high as he could count, he promptly raised his hand above his head and counted to five again.

Did you hear about the Aggie who spent two hours on the phone trying to dial ESTABLISHED 1894?

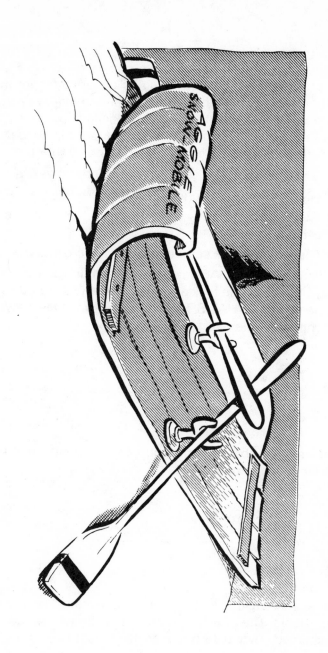

At a recent sports event the Aggies' cheerleader got sick. A rather nervous substitute from a small college was quickly drafted. Determined to do well, he looked up at the stands packed with cheering Aggies, cleared his throat and shouted, "Give me an F!" "F," the crowd shouted.

"Give me an I!" he yelled. "I," the crowd yelled.

"Give me a G!" he cried. "G," the crowd cried.

"Give me and H!" he screamed. "H," the crowd screamed.

"Give me a T!" he screeched. "T," the crowd screeched.

Pleased that the Aggies were responding so well on the very first cheer, he took a deep breath and shouted as loud as he could, "WHAT'S THAT SPELL?" and was answered by complete silence.

Did you hear about the new parachute developed at Texas A&M? It opens on impact.

An Aggie rang the door bell, and a stark naked lady came to the door. The Aggie pointed his finger at her and exclaimed, "My wife has a costume just like yours!"

Did you hear about the Aggie whose father told him about the birds and the bees. Two days later the Aggie was stung by a bee and he thought he was pregnant.

There was an Aggie who had come to such desperate straits that the only alternative he could see was to kidnap a millionaire's kid. So he found one, about 6, and snatched him. Then the kidnapper wrote a ransom note, signing his name, asking for $500,000 in small bills — but he forgot the address of the millionaire. So he gave the note to the kid and told him to take it to his Dad. This the kid did, and when he returned with the money, there was also a note from the victim: "Here's your filthy money. And I gotta say it's a rotten thing for one Aggie to do to another."

Then there was the Aggie who used some nasal spray and got diarrhea.

What do you find in an Aggie's nose?
   Fingerprints.

Did you hear about the constipated Aggie who worked it out with a slide rule?

The army officer ordered the Aggie private to form a firing squard. "All right, you guys," the Aggie barked," get in a circle."

Do you know how to keep Aggies on their toes?
Raise the urinals.

Then there were the four Aggie sailors who lost their lives. One died at sea, and the other three drowned trying to dig his grave.

An Aggie came home and found his wife in bed with a man. The Aggie stormed across the bedroom, took a gun from a dresser drawer and pointed it at his own head. His wife started laughing. "Don't laugh, sister," he warned her angrily. "You're next!"

Did you hear about the Aggie who saw "Guess Who's Coming to Dinner" twice, and guessed wrong both times?

Do you know why Aggies can't lie on the beach? Cats will bury them.

A T-Sipper began telling an Aggie joke. A man stood up, "Just a minute, I'm an Aggie," "O. K.," said the T-Sipper, "I'll speak slower."

Do you know how an Aggie knows how to put his shorts on? Yellow spot in front, brown spot in back.

Then there was the Aggie math major who had just learned to count to 21, when he was arrested for indecent exposure.

An Aggie was invited to his wealthy girlfriend's home for dinner. When he walked into the house, the butler said: "Cocktails are being served in the library." So he ran all the way downtown.

PANHANDLER: Would you give me 50¢ for a sandwich?
AGGIE: I don't know. Let me see the sandwich.

Did you hear that Texas A&M is recalling thermometers because traces of mercury were found in them?

Did you hear about the Aggie football player who demanded at 50% discount from a chiropractor because he was a halfback?

How do you get an Aggie out of the bathtub? Throw in a bar of soap.

Aggie Birth Certificate: a letter of apology from the Trojan Rubber Co.

Did you hear about the Aggie who thought an innuendo was an Italian suppository?

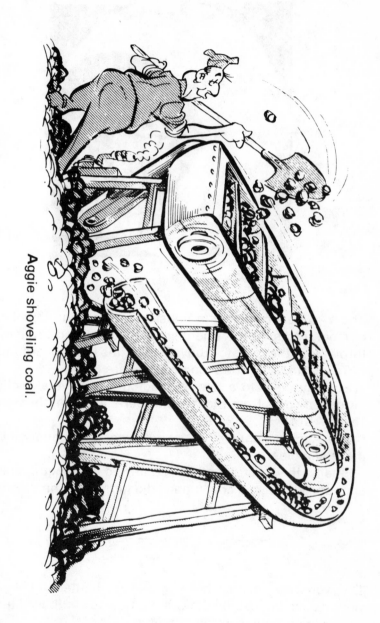

Aggie shoveling coal.

The NASA space center in Houston was sending samples of moon rocks for the scientists at landgrant universities throughout the U. S. to study. By the time they got around to Texas A&M, all the moon rocks were gone.

So they went to a nearby feedlot, took several well-hardened chips from the ground there, and sent them to Texas A&M.

The Aggie scientists just about went crazy analyzing those samples.

Finally they got together, conferred at length, and announced that the cow indeed did jump over the moon.

Did you hear about the Aggie who wanted to be a pharmacist, but couldn't figure out how to get those little prescription bottles in the typewriter.

Two men walking along the street passed beneath a sign in front of a filling station. Unhappily, just at that moment a pigeon on the sign bombed one of the men squarely on the forehead. As he raised his hand to wipe off the mess, his friend stopped him.

"Look out," he said, "you'll get it in your eyes. Just stand still a second while I step into the men's room here and get some toilet paper to wipe you off."

While the soiled one was awaiting his friend's return, an Aggie came along. "Hey," said the newcomer, "you look terrible! Whazzat all over your face?" The unfortunate man explained about the pigeon. "I'm just waiting for my friend to come back with the toilet paper."

"You silly nuts!" the Aggie said, "Don't you know that ole bird'll be miles away by now?"

Did you hear about the Aggie who thought a pole vault was a jockey strap with a lock on it?

The class in Animal Husbandry at A&M was studying reproduction. As a project, the professor assigned three students to take a bull to a nearby farm to service a cow there.

Hours passed, and the students had not returned.

More hours passed, and still the students had not reported back. The worried prof went to the barn. The bull was in the stall; the three Aggies were lying on the ground, battered and bruised, clothes torn, and completely exhausted.

"What happened?" asked the prof. "Did the bull give you trouble?"

"Naw," replied the Aggie spokesman, "he cooperated, but we had an awful time getting the cow on her back."

Contrary to popular belief, an Aggie fetus is not a janitor in a drum.

T-SIPPER: Did you take a bath today?
AGGIE: Why? Is one missing?

Do you know how a gal knows she's in bed with an Aggie? It isn't hard.

After dating about a year, a rather elderly Aggie and a rather elderly lady began to seriously consider getting married. They discussed various likes and dislikes, and the Aggie asked, "How about sex?"

"Infrequently," replied the lady of his affections.

"Is that one word, or two?" asked the Aggie.

Did you hear about the Aggie accountant who went to work for a company and absconded with all the accounts payable?

OUT

AGGIE MAZE

IN

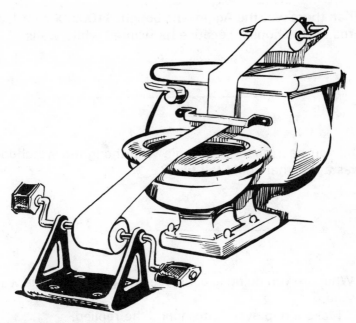

Aggie Paper Recycle
    Pat. Pending
The answer to the paper shortage and the solution to your pollution.

TSIPPER: How did you break your arm?
  AGGIE: I fell out of a tree.
  T-SIPPER: How far did you fall?
  AGGIE: All the way to the ground.

There was an Aggie who always wanted to be a pilot. When he was on his first flight approaching the D/FW airport he called for instructions.
  VOICE OF CONTROL TOWER: "Would you please give us your altitude and position?"
  VOICE OF AGGIE PILOT: "I'm 5 feet 10 inches, and I'm sitting up front."

Then there was the Aggie who bought $100,000 worth of tires for his house, because he wanted white walls.

Did you hear about the Aggie who thought a watchdog was a dog that could tell time?

"What are you doing to conserve energy?" the Aggie was asked.
   "I take a nap every afternoon," he replied.

A freshman Aggie was required to take his first P.E. course. Upon being informed he needed an athletic supporter, he proceeded to the bookstore to purchase one. An Aggie clerk showed him to the back room, pointed to the stacks of boxes marked L, M, and S, and asked, "What size do you need? Long, Medium or short?"

Did you hear what happened to the Aggie who couldn't tell the difference between vaseline and putty?
   His window pane fell out.

Why does an Aggie hold his coffee mug like this? Because that's where the handle is.

T-SIPPER: I'm not working today. Our union went on strike.

AGGIE: Why?

T-SIPPER: We're trying to get shorter hours.

AGGIE: That's a good idea. I always did think 60 minutes was too long for an hour.

An Aggie factory owner pondered over a Federal questionnaire that asked, "How many employees do you have, broken down by sex?" He answered, "None that I know of. Our main problem is alcohol."

Dear Abby:

I have two brothers. One attended Texas A&M. The other was sentenced to the electric chair.

My mother died in the insane asylum when I was three years old. My father is a convicted narcotics pusher. One of my sisters is a highly respected and successful prostitute. The other is the common-law wife of a top Mafia hit man. My uncle is currently serving a life sentence for burglarizing the headquarters of the Boy Scouts of America.

Recently I met a girl shortly after she was released from reform school where she served time for smothering her illegitimate baby. We are very much in love and plan to be married soon. She knows nothing about my family.

My problem is, should I tell her about my brother who attended A&M?

Worried

Did you hear about the Aggie who thought an exorcist was a guy who came to your house to help you get in shape?

In order to get a Peach Bowl bid, Texas Tech had to take 6,000 tickets. This would have been a $45,000 loss, had it not been for two Aggies. They bought the whole lot, so they could scalp 'em.

144

How does an Aggie clean his ears?

Two T-Sippers were standing on a corner waiting for the light to change. An Aggie walked up behind them and stopped. One T-Sipper looked at the other and said, "Do you smell something?" The other T-Sipper said, "Yes, I sure do."

They both turned around and said to the Aggie, "Say, did you have a B.M. in your pants?" The Aggie replied, "I sure did." The T-Sippers said, "Well, why don't you go home and clean them out?" The Aggie said, "I'm not through yet."

An Aggie who had never seen a motorcycle was out walking with his daughter when suddenly a motorcycle came roaring down the street. "Shoot, Pa, Shoot," his daughter exclaimed. The Aggie picked up his rifle and shot five times. "Did you kill it, Pa? Did you?" asked the daughter. "No," the Aggie answered. "It's still growling. But I made it let go of the man it was carrying."

Did you hear about the Aggie who bought a ladder, and carefully put a sign on the top rung: "STOP HERE."

T-SIPPER: What with inflation, the cost of living is so high I'm going to raise my own chickens this year.

AGGIE: Me, too. See these eggs? I'm planting them today.

Did you hear about the Aggie who tried to stand on his hands?

He broke both of them when he stepped on them.

At Houston's Intercontinental Airport, an Aggie who was waiting for his flight weighed himself on a "Your Weight and Fate" scale. The message read, "You are a 22 year-old Aggie, and when you step off the scales you are going to pass gas." The Aggie stepped off the scales, and sure enough, he passed gas.

He sat down in the waiting room as people glared at him. Red-faced with embarrassment, he muttered to himself. "Surely that was a coincidence. Couldn't happen again in a thousand years. Believe I'll weigh again." Again the message read, "You are a 22 year-old Aggie, and when you step off the scales you are going to pass gas." And again, as he stepped off the scales he passed gas.

Aghast, the Aggie stepped on the scales again, put his last penny in the slot, and this time the message read, "You are a 22 year-old Aggie, and you've farted around and missed your flight."

FIRST AGGIE: My date kissed me last night.
SECOND AGGIE: Did you kiss her back?
FIRST AGGIE: No, I kissed her mouth.

And there was the Aggie employee who won his company's $25 award contest for the best suggestion on how the company could save money. He suggested the amount be cut to $10.

Did you hear about the Aggie who was so obnoxious that when he talks to his plants they turn away?

During deer season a far-sighted Aggie and his friend went hunting. The Aggie heard a crackle, swung around and shot into the brush, wounding his friend. Several hours later at the city hospital the Aggie saw the doctor who tried to save his friend's life. "Your friend would have pulled through," the doctor said bluntly, "if you hadn't gutted him."

An Aggie and a T-Sipper were guests at a wedding reception. "I can't toast the bride, because I'm out of beer," the T-Sipper said. "I thought you used an electric hot plate for that," remarked the Aggie.

Two Aggies were playing golf when the first one said, "Gosh, I have to crap." The second Aggie said, "Well, there's a tree. Go behind it and do your stuff." The first Aggie replied, "But I don't have toilet paper." The second Aggie said, "You have a dollar don't you? Just use it."

Reluctantly the first Aggie went behind the tree and came back several minutes later, covered with crap.

"What happened?" the second Aggie asked. "Didn't you use the dollar?"

"Hell, yes," the first Aggie answered. "But did you ever try to wipe with three quarters, two dimes and a nickel?"

An Aggie and a T-Sipper went to the men's room. The T-Sipper finished first, and left. The Aggie finished, and after washing his hands, met the T-Sipper outside. "At Texas A&M they teach us to wash our hands after we go to the toilet," he commented. "At the University of Texas they teach us not to go to the bathroom on our hands," replied the T-Sipper.

Seven Port-O-Lets stacked on top of each other is an Aggie condominium.

The T-Sipper approached St. Peter at the gate to heaven. St. Peter greeted him warmly, and said, "Welcome to Heaven. We have a simple entrance exam here. Spell God." The T-Sipper said, "G-O-D." "Fine, come on in," St. Peter said.

A Mustang approached. St. Peter explained the simple entrance exam. "Spell God." The Mustang said, "G-O-D."

Then the Aggie came. "We have a simple entrance exam here in heaven," said St. Peter, "Spell Nacogdoches."

A man pulled into a gas station which was run by an Aggie and asked him to check to see if his blinker was working. The Aggie bent down, looked, and said, "Yes . . . No . . . Yes . . . No . . . Yes . . ."

And then there was the daredevil Aggie who jumped 21 Honda Motorcycles with a Mack truck.

Did you hear about the Aggie who thought Emory Bellard was something to file your fingernails with?

An Aggie went hunting and shot two deer. When he went to a taxidermist, he was asked if he wanted them mounted. "No," the Aggie replied, "kissing will be fine."

T-SIPPER TO AGGIE: You've travelled all over the world. Tell me, how do those Italian and French dishes compare to our American dishes?

AGGIE: Well, I don't rightly know. They all break about the same.

An Aggie went to an Aggie doctor to find out why urine is yellow and semen is white. "So you can tell whether you're coming or going," the Aggie M.D. told him.

Did you hear about the Aggie who thought graffiti was a highly seasoned pasta dish.

Two Aggies in College Station wanted to go to the S.M.U. game in Dallas, but had no way of getting there. They decided to go to a used car lot and buy a car. "We need a car, but we don't have much money," they told the salesman. "We have a model over here I can let you have for $200," the salesman replied. The Aggies then confessed, "We only have $25 between us." The salesman said, "Well, all I have for $25 is an old camel; just give him a little water and he'll go a long way."

The Aggies bought it, and were on their way to Dallas. As they pulled into the Cotton Bowl parking lot, they heard the attendant say, "Look at those two assholes on that camel." During the game the Aggies realized they had forgotten where they parked the camel. One Aggie asked the other, "How are we going to find our camel?" The other Aggie replied, "Easy, just look for the one with two assholes on it."

And there was the Aggie who was such a slow reader he had to go back to the optometrist a second time to finish the eye chart.

———————————

Then there was the Aggie who thought a taxidermist was a dentist who worked out of the back seat of a cab.

———————————

T-SIPPER: What do you think of bilingualism?
   AGGIE: I think it's okay, if it's between two consenting adults.

AGGIE: The doctor told me to drink some lemon juice after a hot bath.

T-SIPPER: Did you drink the lemon juice?

AGGIE: No, I haven't finished drinking the hot bath yet.

And there was the Aggie who thought the "Don't Walk" sign on the street corner was a bus company advertisement.

The Aggie baseball coach asked a rookie his best playing position.

"Like this — sorta stooped over," answered the rookie.

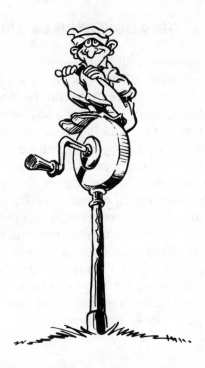

Did you hear about the Aggie who broke his leg at the golf course? He fell off the ball-washing machine.

_____

Do you know how a Senate Subcommittee of Aggies would have handled the Watergate investigation?
  The same way.

_____

Did you hear about the Aggie who called Dial-A-Prayer and they hung up on him?

THE AGGIE STRIKES BACK

One day President Williams received a call from a farmer who wanted to enroll his son with a 180 I.Q. at Texas A&M. President Williams told him he doubted that he or anybody else could do much for a boy with that I. Q., but he had heard of I. Q. reducing facilities at a well known medical center, and suggested that he take his son there and have his I. Q. dropped to 110.

The farmer followed the suggestion, and his son was admitted to the medical center. The boy was placed in the machine, and the I. Q. meter was dropping . . . 170, 160, 150, 140 . . . when suddenly the machine went wild. Before the medical team could get the boy out, his I. Q. had dropped to minus-210. Finally they got the boy out of the machine and waited for him to come out of his coma. The boy regained consciousness, and the first words he uttered were, "Hook 'em Horns!"

―――――――――――

"I just can't find a cause for your illness," the internist said. "Frankly, I think it's due to drinking."

"In that case," replied his Aggie patient, "I'll come back when you're sober."

―――――――――――

An Aggie came home and found his house on fire, rushed next door, telephoned the fire department and shouted, "Hurry over here. My house is on fire." "Okay," the fireman replied. "How do we get there?" "Say," yelled the Aggie, "Don't you still have those big red trucks?"

158

Two Aggies went ice fishing. They caught 300 pounds of ice and got drowned trying to fry it.

The Aggie and his gal were embracing passionately in the front seat. "Want to get in the back seat?" she asked. "No." he said . . . "Now do you want to get in the back seat?" she asked. "No," he replies . . . "NOW do you want to get in the back seat?" she asked. "No," answered the Aggie. "I want to say in the front seat with you."

Did you hear about the Aggie Godfather?
   He'll make you an offer you can't understand.

A slash mark (/) is an Aggie ROTC at attention.

Two Aggies were building a house. One of the Aggies was driving in some of the nails and putting some back in the box. The other Aggie asked why he was doing this. He replied, "The heads are on the wrong end." The second Aggie didn't understand, so the first Aggie explained, "I'll use those for the other side of the house."

Two Aggies, out of town, got drunk and ended up at a party in the home of someone they didn't know. They woke the next morning in their hotel room with considerable hangovers. One said to the other, "That party last night sure was great." "Yes," the other replied, "and I don't believe we thanked the hosts. Let's go back and tell them." The first Aggie said, "Okay, but all I remember is that the house had a gold commode."

After knocking on practically every door in town and asking everyone what color commode they had and getting some very curt replies, they came to the last house on the street. "Do you have a gold commode?" they asked pleasantly. The woman who answered the doorbell, turned around and yelled, "Harry, we found the guy who doo-dooed in the tuba!"

Did you hear about the Aggie who thought pantyhose was what you watered underwear with?

And the Aggie who heard that ice fishing was fun. He was standing on a frozen lake, casting on the ice. He kept reeling the line back off the ice without any success. His Aggie friend came up and asked if he was having any luck. He said, "Hell, no. The fish you aren't biting." "Well," the friend said, "I'll tell you what — we'll go get my snowmobile and troll a while."

Did you hear about the Aggie who sat up all night on his wedding night, waiting for the swelling to go down?

Then there was the Aggie who thought the center of gravity was the letter V.

Did you hear about the Aggie who designed the coolest submarine? It was a screen door.

Don't knock it. It keeps the fish out.

A Texas Tech student and an Aggie were walking along when the Techsan took a breath of air and almost strangled. "Dang," he shouted, "Did you crap in your pants, Aggie?" "No, I didn't," replied the Aggie. "Are you sure?" questioned the Techsan. "I'm sure," said the Aggie. "Are you lying, Aggie?" asked the Techsan. "No I'm not lying," the Aggie answered. "Well, I think I'd better see for myself if you're not," said the Techsan, pulling down the Aggie's pants. "Y-e-e-c-c-h! They're covered with crap, Aggie. I thought you said you didn't crap in your pants," the Techsan exclaimed. "Oh," said the Aggie, starting to grin. "I thought you meant today."

And there's the Aggie who thought ball-joint suspension was the closing of the Chicken Ranch.

And there's the Aggie who won't use toothpaste because he doesn't have any loose teeth.

Did you hear about the Aggie who moved his house closer to the street to take up the slack in his clothesline?

A preacher announced from the pulpit, "Everybody in this congregation will one day die." An Aggie laughed loudly, annoying the preacher who called out, "What do you find so amusing?" The Aggie replied, "I'm not from this congregation."

AGGIE: What's that long rope for?
COWBOY: That's for catching cows.
AGGIE: That's interesting. What do you use for bait?

An Aggie, a T-Sipper and a Sooner were survivors on a wrecked ship in the middle of the ocean. When a helicopter came to rescue them, the pilot said, "There's only room for two. The two who answer my questions correctly can come aboard."

The first question was to the Sooner: "What was the famous ship that went down when it hit an iceberg?" "The Titanic," the Sooner replied.

Next he asked the T-Sipper, "How many people died on it?" "1,517," the T-Sipper answered.

The third question was to the Aggie: "Name them," the pilot asked.

An Aggie hitchhiker was picked up by a guy in a big Lincoln-Continental. The Aggie noticed a bunch of golf tees on the front seat and asked, "What are those things for?"

"They're to hold my balls while I drive," the man answered.

"Boy," exclaimed the Aggie, "these Lincoln-Continentals have everything, don't they?"

Did you hear about the Aggie who robbed a bank? He tied up the safe and blew up the guard.

The Aggie came in from his morning classes, flopped down on his bed and said to his roommate, "I'm bushed. I'm going to sleep a while, but I have a 2 p.m. class, so I can't sleep very long." Just before falling asleep he asked his roommate, "Are you going to be here for a while?" On receiving an affirmative reply, the Aggie said, "That's good. I'll let you know if I want you to awaken me."

T-SIPPER: Do you know how deep that river is?

AGGIE: It must be pretty shallow. It's only up to that duck's stomach.

The city of Houston paints a large W on the sides of its old garbage trucks, ships them to A&M and sells them as Winnebagos.

QUESTION: What does an Aggie say before picking his nose?
ANSWER: Grace.

Did you hear about the Aggie who tried to blow up the school bus?
He burned his lips on the exhaust pipe.

Then there was the Aggie's wife who threw away her pills and diaphragm when her husband told her he had bought a condominium.

Seven-course dinner at Texas A&M: Possum and a six-pack.

A T-Sipper and an Aggie engaged in a punting contest. The T-Sipper's ball went 25 yards; the Aggie's went only 20 yards.

"I won," the T-Sipper exclaimed.

"Shucks, that was nothing," the Aggie replied. "Wait till I use both feet."

———————————

Did you hear about the Aggie who didn't know how to make the number 11?

He didn't know which 1 came first.

———————————

The Aggie martini: A Pearl with a booger in it.

Three fellows were walking down the street. One was an Aggie. The first fellow walked by, snapping his fingers, saying, "I got the beat. I got the beat." The second walked by, snapping his fingers, saying, "I got the beat. I got the beat." Then the Aggie walked by, snapping his fingers. The other two fellows asked him, "Have you got the beat?" "No," the Aggie answered, "I'm trying to get this booger off my finger."

Did you hear about the Aggie chiropodist who always started off on the wrong foot?

A monkey took up residence with an Aggie and followed him everywhere. He asked a friend if he had any suggestions as to what he should do with the monkey. "Call City Hall and ask them," the friend replied. When the Aggie called City Hall, they suggested that he take the monkey to the Zoo. The next day the friend saw the Aggie with the monkey and said, "Didn't you call City Hall?" "Yes," said the Aggie, "and they told me to take it to the Zoo, so I did, and he enjoyed it so much that today I'm taking him to Six Flags."

Do you know how to tell an Aggie Santa Claus? He's the one with the Easter basket.

The Aggie soldier was guarding the main gate at the base. His orders were to keep cars out, unless they had a special sticker on the windshield.

A big car drove up to the gate; a general was sitting in the back. "Halt, who goes there?" the Aggie asked. The general's driver said, "General Davis."

"I'm sorry," the Aggie replied. "I cannot let you through. You don't have the right kind of sticker on the windshield." The general said to his driver, "Go on, drive through."

The Aggie said, "I'm really sorry, but I have orders to shoot anyone who tries to drive through without a sticker." The general said to his driver, "Stop wasting time, driver, go on."

The Aggie walked over to the rear window of the car and said, "General, I'm new at this. Whom do I shoot? You or the driver?"

Did you hear about the two Aggies who went into the loan shark business? They lent out all their money and then skipped town.

A man and his wife, both of whom were Yankees were motoring through Texas. When they reached Mexia, an argument ensued as to the correct pronunciation. The husband insisted on pronouncing the x — the wife equally sure that h was correct. The husband said, "There's one way to settle this. We'll ask a native. Let's stop here for lunch."

The waiter was an Aggie. "Would you mind slowly pronouncing the name of this place?" asked the husband. The Aggie replied, "No, sir. D-A-I-R-Y Q-U-E-E-N."

We are the Aggies,
The Aggies we are.
We ain't as dumb
As you think we is.

T.G.I.F. printed on Aggies' shoes does not mean "Thank God It's Friday." It stands for, "Toes Go In First."

Here's the way the Aggie football coach decides what positions his players will play. He puts them in the forest. The ones who run over trees are linemen; the ones who run around the trees are backs.

The Aggies have invented a birth control pill for men. Worn in their shoes — makes 'em limp.

Tact: a pointy thing you drive in the wall to hang an Aggie diploma on.

Did you hear about the Aggie who is such a slow reader he leaves placemarks in newspapers?

Did you hear about the Aggie who died from eating mountain oysters?

He was dragged to death by a bull.

An Aggie had been celebrating a little too much after a football game. When he got back to his hotel lobby, he leaned on one of the elevator doors. Suddenly the doors came open, and he fell into the elevator pit. He stumbled to his feet, brushed himself off, and said, "I said up, dammit!"

Did you hear about the Aggie square dancer who thought do-se-do was money on display?

Did you hear about the Aggie who used his credit card to make an obscene phone call?

Then there was the Aggie who played Russian roulette with a derringer.

AGGIE JOKES . . . PRO AND CON

As the foreword to this book indicates, we're now 11 years into publishing in printed form the best of probably a couple of thousand Aggie Jokes we've heard over that time.

A big question we get is "How do the Aggies like them?" Back in the early days, they didn't laugh very much when a new book came out. Now, it appears they're softening because they've asked our permission to include some of our jokes and cartoons in their current yearbook.

Sales in College Station and Bryan continue to lead the other cities we sell in — meaning one of two things. Aggies are either buying them in huge lots to fuel their annual A&M/UT bonfire or they're enjoying them. We hope the latter.

The Aggies have been good to the three of us in this little fun, side venture. We hope they give us some credit for their record-breaking enrollment year after year.

Oops . . . we'd better leave while we're ahead. Hope you enjoy the book!

The Publishers

Use these coupons

to order copies of

AGGIE JOKES

for your friends

ORDER FORM

Clip and mail the coupons below to:
The Gigem Press
P. O. Box 64445
Dallas, Texas 75206

- — — — — — — — — — — — — — — — — — — —

Please send:

_____Best of 606 Aggie Jokes @ $4.95

_____Vol. 1 _____Vol. 2 _____Vol. 3 _____Vol. 4

_____Vol. 5 _____Vol. 6 _____Vol. 7 _____Vol. 8

at $1.25 plus Sales Tax. Check or money order must accompany order. Books will be mailed with postage paid.

Name _____

Address _____

City _____ **State** _____ **Zip** _____

- — — — — — — — — — — — — — — — — — — —

Please send:

_____Best of 606 Aggie Jokes @ $4.95

_____Vol. 1 _____Vol. 2 _____Vol. 3 _____Vol. 4

_____Vol. 5 _____Vol. 6 _____Vol. 7 _____Vol. 8

at $1.25 plus Sales Tax. Check or money order must accompany order. Books will be mailed with postage paid.

Name _____

Address _____

City _____ **State** _____ **Zip** _____

- — — — — — — — — — — — — — — — — — — —

Please send:

_____Best of 606 Aggie Jokes @ $4.95

_____Vol. 1 _____Vol. 2 _____Vol. 3 _____Vol. 4

_____Vol. 5 _____Vol. 6 _____Vol. 7 _____Vol. 8

at $1.25 plus Sales Tax. Check or money order must accompany order. Books will be mailed with postage paid.

Name _____

Address _____

City _____ **State** _____ **Zip** _____